"Kenneth and Mark move from theory to pr... ...is
book on church revit... ...
showing a church ho...
churches need to rea...

Jim Richar...
Texas Conventio...

"Every Pastor must be a leader. Leadership requires taking risks. In *Rubicons of Revitalization*, Clifton and Priest address eight key Rubicons, which are points of no return for every pastor and church. Pastors are encouraged to wade into the water with a mindset to not turn back especially as it relates to gospel advance. If your church is in need of revitalization, this book is essential for you as a pastor to consider what Rubicons are you facing. Let me encourage you to wade out into the water for the sake of the gospel."

Ronnie Floyd, *Senior Pastor, Cross Church; President, National Day of Prayer; Past President, Southern Baptist Convention*

In *Rubicons of Revitalization* Mark Clifton and Kenneth Priest offer hope to pastors and churches intent on experiencing revival and revitalization. In this book, pastors and congregations are encouraged to advance through and beyond the Rubicons, or boundaries, that have prevented their spiritual and physical growth to occur through Prayer, Preaching, Evangelism, Discipleship, Leadership, Programs, Polity, and Facilities. As a former pastor who revitalized a declining congregation and now a professor who teaches church revitalization, I wholeheartedly recommend this book and its principles.

Matt Queen, *L. R. Scarborough Chair of Evangelism ("The Chair of Fire"); Associate Professor of Evangelism; Southwestern Baptist Theological Seminary, Fort Worth, Texas*

This book hits the bullseye! While many aspects of church life are important for church revitalization, Mark Clifton and Kenneth Priest bring to the surface most crucial areas churches must embrace in order to see a new movement of God among them. If you are looking to have a ministry on cruise control, this book is not for you. However, if you desire to see God transform your church and community, this book is a must read! I wholeheartedly recommend you read this, apply it, and then hold on as God does a new work among you!

Nathan Lorick, *Executive Director, Colorado Baptist General Convention*

RUBICONS

of revitalization

overcoming 8 common barriers to church renewal

Mark Clifton
+ Kenneth Priest

RUBICONS OF REVITALIZATION

TABLE OF CONTENTS

On my part I dedicate this book to the elders at the Wornall Road Baptist Church in Kansas City, Missouri. It was while working among those elders that God revealed to me his love for dying churches and it was where I learned much of what I now know as key strategies to church revitalization.

– Mark Clifton

On my part, I dedicate this work to the pastors engaged in revitalization across Texas whom I have the privilege of serving in my role with the Southern Baptists of Texas Convention. The ministry of revitalization in our state would not be, if it were not for each one of you.

– Kenneth Priest

ACKNOWLEDGMENTS

We want to thank Judi Hayes for her work as our editor on this project. Her insights are always beneficial and appreciated. We thank Kevin Ezell and the North American Mission Board where Mark serves and Kenneth is a trustee for championing the cause of replanting and revitalization across North America. Additionally, we have great gratitude for Jason Allen and Midwestern Baptist Theological Seminary where both Mark and Kenneth serve in adjunct roles teaching and equipping in replanting and revitalization. These opportunities in academia challenge us to create resources such as this writing.

I express gratitude to my wife, Jill, for her encouragement and all of my ministry and in particular her encouragement for me to commit my time and energy to writing. I also want to express gratitude to the amazing Replant team at the North American Mission Board. This group of men continue to encourage me in every aspect of my work and ministry. They are not only among my dearest friends, but they are my most valuable ministry colleagues.

– Mark Clifton

First, I want to express my personal gratitude to Debbi, my wife. Her constant input and feedback in ministry is truly iron sharpening iron for the ministry which God has placed us in. Her encouragement for me to write and provide final edits on manuscripts is what makes the work you are reading possible I have additional gratitude to Jim Richards and the Southern Baptists of Texas Convention. His encouragement to help the church, no matter what church, whenever called upon is why I came to the SBTC in 2008. I give special thanks to Mike and Connie Landry as they have joined the ministry in Texas where Mike serves as a consultant to the SBTC in revitalization. His partnership in gospel work and passion for the expansion of the kingdom is contagious and his heart for the church perfectly positions him to serve in Texas and Connie as she encourages pastor wives along the way; thanks to both of you.

– Kenneth Priest

FOREWORD

From the time that I graduated from seminary, an aura existed that seemed to pressure pastors into believing that they should be personally planting churches. Most of the pastors I know and my seminary contemporaries all believed that, in order to reach America, we needed to be planting more churches. Within the last few decades, as the church planting movement accelerated, the pressure to be a planting pastor increased. Many pastors launched out into the church planting abyss, only to find themselves shipwrecked and drowning. Their demise came, not because of a lack of training, character, or passion, but simply because their skill sets and spiritual giftings did not match those needed to successfully plant a church. In recent years, in my own denomination, church planters are required to go through a rigorous assessment process to determine if a candidate genuinely has the gifting to be a successful planter. I am thankful that we are realizing that not everyone is called or gifted to plant a church. As a result, I believe our church planting efforts have become far more prolific than in years past.

The same perspective holds true for church revitalization. In 2016, Mark Clifton wrote a book entitled *Reclaiming Glory: Revitalizing Dying Churches*. In that book, Clifton listed eight characteristics for being an effective church revitalizer. Just like with church planting, revitalizing a church requires more than just an opportunity or even a desire. A certain skill set, spiritual gifting, and personal attitudes toward the church all play into the role of an effective revitalizer.

Mark Clifton and Kenneth Priest have now provided an outstanding addition to these necessary revitalization skills. *Rubicons of Revitalization* is more than just another list of practical steps for the church and pastor to take in order to experience revitalization. The book lays out eight standards – Rubicons – that cannot be ignored or dismissed. While we understand the necessary requirements for revitalizing a church, I think we pastors often overlook or underestimate the importance of one or more of these Rubicons. As Caesar stepped into the Rubicon River as an act of defiance and as a declaration of war, for us to fail to cross any of these boundaries analogously pushes us into a seemingly denial of the sufficiency of Scripture and the Sovereignty of God. I make that statement with those qualifications because I cannot imagine any pastor of character volitionally standing in rebellion against our Lord. I do know, however, that we can get so caught up in our methodologies, our conflicts, our fears, and our personalities that we sometimes overlook the work of the Holy Spirit. Clifton and Priest call us back to a pivotal dependence on God to bring about church revitalization. In that utter dependence, we must demonstrate the courage to press on into the waters of a spiritual warfare that takes back our churches from the clutches of death. Not everyone is perhaps gifted to be a church revitalizer. Those who are, though, must have the courage and perseverance to step into the waters of these eight Rubicons.

These are more than just principles. These are lines drawn in the sand.

A few years ago, I was invited to present a paper on conflict in the church. The obvious reason conflict exists is because we are Genesis 3 people. We are sinners, and even now as the redeemed, we battle with the flesh. A secondary reason that is much associated with the first is spiritual warfare. Churches have conflict and decline because they are in the midst of an oftentimes misunderstood and unseen spiritual battle. A tertiary cause, though just as prevalent, is the presence of spiritual and physical Rubicons. Though I did not state them as such in the paper (and wish I had since the Rubicon is such a great parallelism), churches hit the plateau and begin to decline because they set up boundaries in leadership, polity, process, and mission that lead to power struggles, a disconnect between church and community, and internal conflicts toward change. If they do not cross these Rubicons, the church is on its way to death.

Clifton and Priest offer an incredible challenge to pastors of churches in need of revitalization or ones considering this ministry. Being a revitalization pastor is not for the faint of heart. One must be willing to endure hardship, criticism, and cynicism in order to bring about the necessary changes churches must embrace so that they can revitalize.

This book is an essential read for all pastors. It is also a reminder of why pastors and churches must see themselves as members of the same team. We are not the enemy. The enemy has set up Rubicons that appeal to the flesh. He allures us through the lust of the flesh, the lust of the eyes, and the pride of life. Therefore, we set up boundaries that stifle the church and quench the Spirit. The answer to these dilemmas is to cross over these Rubicons and declare war on the true enemy of the church. And when the church does, she must never look back.

Bill Henard, *Executive Director-Treasurer, The West Virginia Convention of Southern Baptists*

INTRODUCTION

Rubicon: a bounding or limiting line; especially: one that when crossed commits a person irrevocably

In 49 B.C., Julius Caesar led his army to the banks of the Rubicon, a small river that marked the boundary between Italy and Gaul. Caesar knew Roman law forbade a general from leading his army out of the province to which he was assigned. By crossing the Rubicon, he would violate that law. "The die is cast," he said, wading in. That act of defiance sparked a three-year civil war that ultimately left Julius Caesar the undisputed ruler of the Roman world. It also inspired English speakers to adopt two popular sayings—*crossing the Rubicon* and *the die is cast*—centuries later. *Rubicon* has been used in English as the name of a significant figurative boundary since at least the early 1600s.[1]

Organizations ultimately reach a boundary line, an arbitrary limiting factor that prevents them from moving forward. This is true for the church as well. These limiting lines can occur in various ways. What we are attempting to communicate in this writing are the Rubicons of Revitalization. There are boundaries for each of the Rubicons; likewise, there are opportunities to commit and push past the boundaries. Once this is done, you must proceed forward with your plan for revitalization and not turn back. Just as Julius Caesar waded into the water, understanding this was a movement to war, which lasted three years, when a pastor leads his church into the Rubicon waters of these issues, he is committing to take the church on a journey for renewal and revitalization. The benefits may not be seen for at least three years. Will you wade into these waters? Or will you turn and go back, allowing the Rubicon water to flow without the stirring of your footsteps?

Rubicon 1: Prayer

A classic definition of Christian prayer is "an offering up of our desires unto God, for things agreeable to his will, in the name of Christ, with confession of our sins, and thankful acknowledgement of his mercies" (Westminster Shorter Catechism).[2] *The Rubicon of prayer is when prayer has become a demands or expectation list for God.* It is the rote process of communicating to God, but not really communicating with God.

Rubicon 2: Preaching

In the New Testament, preaching is "the public proclamation of Christianity to the non-Christian world."[3] It is not religious discourse to a closed group of initiates, but open and public proclamation of God's redemptive activity in and through Jesus Christ.[4] *The Rubicon of preaching is a lack of expositional, biblical preaching of the gospel contextualized for the church's community.*

Rubicon 3: Evangelism

To evangelize is to proclaim the good news of the victory of God's salvation. Evangelism is the noun denoting that activity. This biblical concept is expressed through a Hebrew verb (*bāśar*) and a Greek verb and noun (*euangelizō* and *euangelion*). Euangelion is normally translated gospel, denoting the content of the good news. It can also be a noun of action, describing the activity of telling that news.[5] *The Rubicon of evangelism is the failure of the church to reach people for Christ*, the process of believers in the local church sharing their faith in Christ with others.

Rubicon 4: Discipleship

For the Christian this refers to the process of learning the teachings of Jesus and following His example in obedience through the power of the Holy Spirit. Discipleship not only involves the process of becoming a disciple, but of making other disciples through teaching and evangelism.[6] *The Rubicon of discipleship is the failure of the church to mature believers in the faith* to the extent of equipping them to pass on their legacy of faith to those with whom are living the Christian life.

Rubicon 5: Leadership

Church leadership refers to those who belong to the church of God and who are set apart in order to lead and direct the affairs of the church, following the example set by the paragon of servant leaders, Jesus Christ. Church leadership is varied in terms of role and function, though not limited by gender or race, and expressed as a result of the corporate discernment and affirmation of the church.[7] *The Rubicon of leadership* can develop in several ways, one of which is those presently in leadership *failing to pass along leadership to the emerging generations.* Another is simply *not developing yourself as a leader* by continuing to learn best practices for your area of leadership.

Rubicon 6: Programs

Church program ministries provide the framework for which a church performs ministry in its context. These ministries address various life-stage discipling opportunities along with activities for caring for the church as a whole and the larger community where the church is positioned. *The Rubicon of programs is when more emphasis is placed on the programs of the church and their respective ministries than on gospel advance* within the community. Therefore, a church would sacrifice witness over ministry.

Rubicon 7: Polity

Church polity essentially describes how the church governance will function. Examples of this include whether the church will have elders, whether the congregation is pastor led or committee led, what role the deacons should play in leading the church, etc. *The Rubicon of polity is allowing structure to mandate function of the church instead of God's Word.* At a point of tension, instead of biblically addressing conflict, the Rubicon of polity champions other methods diverting from God's Word.

Rubicon 8: Facilities

The property and grounds of a church control curb appeal. *The Rubicon of facilities diverts budget from maintenance needs on the property* with an idea of "we will handle it next year." The problem with this Rubicon is that next year never comes. A church can cross the point of no return in delayed maintenance, where it becomes more cost effective to walk away from the property, or certain buildings of the property, as bringing them up-to-date is no longer cost effective.

The Die Is Cast

As Julius Caesar stepped into the Rubicon River, he was certain of one thing: he could not turn back. He had intentionally stepped into war. His motives appeared to be that of self-preservation in leadership. Politically he was astute. As such, he maneuvered his career strategically making alliances and decisions which benefited and protected him. He was seen as being "of the people," which gave him impressive influence.

As you think about revitalizing a church, the first decision should be, Do you wade into the waters of your Rubicon? No, this is not an issue of war per se, but it is an issue of spiritual warfare. Certain realities will be raised to the surface based on your decision to wade into the waters. The most difficult part of wading in is knowing you could lose your job over this. Pastor, are you ready for this? If so, then the die is cast. Step into the Rubicon facing you and begin your journey.

Some may think the reality of losing a job over stepping into the Rubicon is a scare tactic. However, we have seen this time and again. Here are the realities; several things could happen in the midst of wading in the water. As you wade in, you may discover those around you are not ready or not onboard with what God is leading you to do. In fact, you may discover such complacency and inability to attract new people due to the existing personalities so that you cannot overcome the quagmire that has been created. In these times a pastor has to ask himself, "Should I even stay?" Allowing God the opportunity to move you into other waters may mean a transition is in your future. The other possibility is that the existing ego of church leaders cannot handle the direction you are trying to lead, and they force your termination. The difference in the two is this: option one is God's movement in your life to protect you from a group of persons not focused on His will. The second option is a people of God who are being disobedient to the work of the Lord.

The next option is this: you wade in the waters, and the congregation joins you in this journey of renewal. Whereas in the first two options, whether of God or of man, the church is not ready to move, in this option they are. From here revitalization can occur. As the leader, you are now charged with pushing through for the cause of Christ. Your calling is to lead the people; therefore, you must step up and lead with humility and determination. You cannot turn back once you have determined to cross your church's Rubicon(s).

RUBICON 1: PRAYER

As I've traveled around the country talking to leaders who are a part of revitalization efforts, I've seen God do great work in many churches. I've seen God do what only He can do.

I've seen one common bond in all of these efforts though. All of their work and decision making centered around prayer.

Nothing happens in a dying church until we learn to pray. John Piper often calls prayer "war-time communication." And without a doubt you desperately need wartime communication when you're in the midst of revitalizing a dying church—*because it's certainly a war.*

As you already know from the introduction, a Rubicon is a boundary. So you are likely wondering, *How can prayer be a boundary to anything?*

Prayer itself may perhaps not be a Rubicon, but how we treat prayer sets a boundary in church revitalization. Your activity as a church leader can't revitalize a church. Only the activity of God through the Holy Spirit can regenerate hearts and bring people from death to life. Without a shadow of a doubt, only the Spirit of God can revitalize a church.

Remember the story in John 2 about Jesus's turning water into wine? He told the servants to fill the jars with water. The Gospel writer says those servants filled the jars to the brim. They put every ounce of water they could in there and measured carefully. At the end of all of that, it was just water.

The water didn't become wine until Jesus acted.

Don't get me wrong. Our activity matters. God was pleased to use the servants to fill the jars. He didn't need them to do so, but it pleased Him.

Serving and working in the revitalization of our churches is a privilege. All of our effort doesn't accomplish anything in and of itself. It's still water when the wedding needs wine. Jesus turns water to wine. We can't.

For all of the work we do, none of it makes a difference without the power of the Holy Spirit, and that comes when we pray. Scripture makes abundantly clear that when God's people pray, God moves.

When the first-century church encountered persecution, they stopped and prayed. When the apostle Paul is in prison and can't go anywhere, he prays. If the New Testament church thought prayer was that important, we should too. A lack of prayer is a serious boundary to revitalization. Five specific aspects of our prayer lives will limit our revitalization efforts.

We Pray Too Little

When you compare the hours our churches spend planning, promoting, dealing with budgets, having committee meetings, having town hall meetings, going to conferences, reading books, and watching videos, the time we spend in prayer pales in comparison.

While I was replanting Wornall Road Baptist Church in Kansas City, we experienced many struggles in the early years. If you had asked me, "Hey, are you praying?" I would have said yes. I wasn't praying nearly enough.

At one point I was discipling a young Christian who was passionate for Jesus. One Thursday night he asked if we could meet to pray after he put his kids to bed. So we did. We met at the church, got on our knees, and prayed. He prayed for me. I prayed for him. We prayed together for the church. We just kept praying and praying that night. Not long after that night, we invited another young man to join us. Then we invited another. As we gathered to pray over an extended period of time, God began to bring life back into that church.

Most of the people in our churches don't know how to pray more than just a few minutes. We've grown accustomed limiting prayer to thanking God for the food and asking Him to protect us. We can't fathom praying for forty-five minutes. Most Christians won't do it.

The adversary knows that. He doesn't want us to pray.

When I'm teaching people how to pray more frequently and longer, I recommend praying through Scripture. Take a psalm and read a few verses of that psalm. If those truths in that verse apply to your heart, then thank God for those truths. If the verses remind you of something you're lacking, ask God to bring that to you. You can even take out a hymnal and open it up to one of the great hymns. Read a line from it and stop to thank God for that truth. Learn to pray through Scripture, hymns, and even modern worship songs. Before you know it, you will have spent forty-five minutes to an hour in prayer.

We Pray Too Late

When we're in the midst of revitalization, we do everything before we pray. We go to conferences. We talk to other pastors. We make big plans. Sometimes we even start carrying out those plans. Then, almost as an afterthought, we pray. Prayer is rarely the first thing we do. Most of the time, it's our last resort.

We should pray before we ever get started. The time to pray is before we even begin to plan. The time to pray is when you're at the beginning, as soon as you realize your church needs to be revitalized.

Henry Blackaby has often said, "Well, don't you sit there. Do something." I've heard that all my life. You have, too. Henry would also say, "If you haven't heard a word from God and you don't know what you're supposed to do, don't just go do something. Sit there and pray until you get that word." That's what I'm suggesting we need to do in revitalization.

Don't wait until you've started the work to pray. If you wait to pray, you'll already have a whole host of problems and difficulties by the time you start praying.

Don't pray last. Pray first. Pray first and pray frequently.

We Pray Too Timidly

In the book of 1 Timothy, the apostle Paul wrote to a discouraged young Timothy. We know Timothy wants to quit because early in the book (1 Tim. 1:3) Paul urges him not to leave Ephesus. He was facing all kinds of problems in the church—doctrinal, relational, and generational. Paul spends most of the first chapter of the letter building up young Timothy, reminding him of his calling.

Then, as he begins chapter 2, Paul gets really practical. Paul tells Timothy to start his work in prayer. Paul doesn't ask this small, dysfunctional church in modern Turkey to pray for their church, their family, or even for their little corner of the Roman Empire.

Paul tells the church to pray for the whole world! He urges them to pray huge, bodacious prayers. Clearly I think God wanted this struggling church to understand they serve a big, bodacious God.

Churches in the midst of revitalization shouldn't think small, and they shouldn't pray small either. (Frankly, small thinking and small praying are probably why they're dying in the first place.)

Think about that prayer of the small struggling church in Ephesus. (Read 1 Timothy 2:1 as a reminder of what Paul urged Timothy to pray.) Today, two thousand years later, God has answered it. The gospel is all around this globe. The sun never sets on missionaries and preachers who proclaim the good news of Jesus Christ.

So let's not pray timidly. The adversary wants to keep our prayers timid. We need prayers as big as the great big majestic God we serve.

We Pray Too Few Prayers of Repentance

This is big. Maybe we should have started with it. How often do we pray for repentance in public worship services? Not nearly enough.

When I was at Wornall, we prayed every Sunday morning that our hearts would receive the gospel. It was a prayer of repentance where we acknowledged our sin and hardness of heart.

Prayers of true repentance aren't just big blanket prayers. It's not about asking the Lord to forgive us of everything we've done wrong. In real prayers of repentance, individually and corporately, we acknowledge specific sins in our lives, confess them, and turn from them.

We don't need to avoid repentance. It's a wonderful fountain we should run to every day. It's glorious to repent, confess our sin, and be clean again. The apostle John tells us, "If we confess our sins, he is faithful and just to forgive us our sins and to cleanse us from all unrighteousness" (1 John 1:9). We should want to drink from that fountain every day.

Often our prayers of repentance are so shallow, superficial, and too far and few between. Instead of these weak prayers of repentance, God urges us to pray with deep sadness for our sin and a deep pleading for God's forgiveness to make us right with Him once again.

We Pray Too Often for What We Want

I'm glad God doesn't give us everything we pray for. If He did, I'd be married to Jan Brady. As a twelve-year-old boy, that's what I prayed for as I watched *The Brady Bunch*.

Unfortunately we spend most of our time in prayer asking for God to give us things—such as a job or a spouse. Even in the church we pray mostly for what *we want to see* happen in the church.

That's inappropriate. We need to be praying for what God wants to happen in our church. We must pray that God will open our eyes in a way *where we want what He wants*. This is critically important in church revitalization.

In Jesus's Model Prayer, He prays, "Thy kingdom come, Thy will be done in earth, as it is in heaven" (Matt. 6:10 KJV). It's what God wants for your church that matters, not what you want.

When the Scripture says God wants to give you the desires of your heart, it doesn't mean He'll give you whatever fleshly desire you have—like cars, wealth, and fame. Instead, He says, if you want what God wants, you'll get it. Prayer needs to focus on seeking what God wants for His church.

The Rubicon of prayer means that prayer can become a boundary to what God will do in our church. When we pray too infrequently, too late, too timidly, too few prayers of repentance, too much of our own agenda, we limit God's work in our churches.

Pastor, before we move on from this topic, think about your public prayers. It's easy to get frustrated at how our congregants pray. Guess what? They've heard you pray more than anyone else.

Think about how you, as a pastor, pray in gathered worship on Sunday mornings, over a potluck meal, at a wedding, at a funeral. What do your congregants hear? Maybe the reason they pray too little, pray too late, pray too timidly, pray too few prayers of repentance, and pray too much for what they want is because they've been listening to you.

Richard Blackaby has said, "How you, as a pastor, pray in public should make anyone in the church say, 'I can't wait to go home and do that.'"

I've also heard Richard ask pastors, "How much time do you spend preparing to talk to your people about God on Sunday morning compared to how little time you spend preparing what you're going to say to God about your people?" It's a convicting question, isn't it?

In most churches your people could almost say the whole offertory prayer and the benedictory prayer before they even hear it. Often our corporate prayers are a stream of worn-out phrases that mean almost nothing to us anymore.

This Sunday, when you have an opportunity to pray the blessing for your potluck lunch at church, don't just pray something generic and off of the top of your head. Don't just thank God for the food, the hands that prepared it, and the fellowship around the meal. No one is really listening when you do that.

Use each prayer as an opportunity, even for a potluck meal, to describe the glory of God and His faithfulness in all things. Don't waste any opportunity to pray in front of your people.

If you really believe prayer will play a critical role in your church's revitalization efforts, model strong biblical prayers for your people. Nothing you do will be more important.

RUBICON 2: PREACHING

During the last forty years of ministry, I've come to believe with all of my heart that the preaching of the Word of God effectually revitalizes a church. It's not all you need to do in revitalization. You'll need to pray, evangelize, serve the community, make disciples, and everything else you're reading about in this book. All of that flows from effectual preaching of God's Word.

Preaching can easily become a Rubicon or a boundary on your church's revitalization work. We limit the activity of God when we don't preach effectively. Only God's Word transforms lives. Only the gospel regenerates a heart and brings a dead man back to life. That's why it's so important for us to pay attention to these boundaries of preaching in revitalization so you're not limiting God along the way.

The Boundary of Bible Bingo

Early in my ministry I was guilty of Bible bingo. I'd pick and choose passages to preach from week to week with little rhyme or reason. I preached whatever I felt like preaching. Usually that meant I'd focus on an easy text. I had no continuity. I'd bounce from one Scripture to another, sometimes even pulling stories and verses out of context to make my point.

I don't want to admit how many times I preached an Old Testament passage by pulling out three or four verses and building a whole sermon around them. Those sermons were completely disconnected from the context of what God was doing in the lives of the Hebrews.

It's not just me though. I know pastors who each week pick a few verses randomly and preach on them. That's why I call it Bible bingo. There's no continuity in it.

If we want God to bring new life to our churches, we must stop preaching simple moralistic sermons by pulling a story out of context week after week. Instead, let's preach all of God's Word.

Let me be clear. You don't have to preach exegetically every Sunday. You may have an occasional Sunday when you preach topically, but you should have enough of a base that your congregants know the difference.

You also don't necessarily need to preach through entire books. For example, I don't recommend you preach through the book of Romans all at once. You'd likely take three or four years to do that right. Instead, preach a few chapters of Romans, then a few Psalms, and then go back to Romans.

Preaching exegetically has three great benefits for churches in the revitalization process.

1. It will develop your preaching. Preaching through portions of the Bible forces you to look at every text and not simply skip the tough ones. It makes you work harder as you preach instead of just preaching the easy texts. That hard work will make you a better preacher over time.

2. Every problem in the church will be revealed. When you preach through the whole Bible, God will shine a light on sin. No one can say you're picking out sin just to single someone out. If you've been in a passage for three weeks and God uses Scripture to point out sin, it's not the pastor—*it's God.*

3. Your people will develop an ear for good preaching. You're training your people to connect the theological dots. That will have a long-lasting impact on their spiritual growth.

The Boundary of Christless Preaching

At one point a wonderful young man in my ministry had been raised a Hindu. I often asked people to critique my sermons and help me preach better. I remember Kumar would often say, "You know, that was good, but my father, who is Hindu, would have agreed with everything you said."

God is good. God loves us. God cares for us. Those statements are all true, but where is Christ in them? God is good to us because He sent Christ. God is able to do all things because we have Christ in us. We must make sure to bring Christ into whatever text we preach. He's already there. We simply need to reveal Him to our people.

I preached my first sermon when I was sixteen years old during youth night at our church. I prepared for hours to preach on David and Goliath. For the most part, I preached it the way I'd heard the story told my whole life, but I was wrong.

God still used it. In His providence and in His grace, God can use our mistakes and make something good out of it.

My version went something like this. Goliath was an obstacle we all face that seems overwhelming. Because of David's faith, God gave him five little rocks and directed those rocks right to Goliath's head.

No one would tell a sixteen-year-old this, but it was awful.

I preached the whole message without bringing Christ into it. My version of David and Goliath wasn't about Jesus. It was all about me. I was the hero. I could defeat any temptation through my own bravery and faith in God.

It's just not true.

I'm not the hero in that story. I'm hiding in the woods. I'm the Israelite army who was too afraid to fight because I knew I didn't stand a chance. The Israelite army was hopeless and needed young David to do what they couldn't.

Do you remember how the story ends? Most people believe it ended with Goliath collapsing after David nailed him with the rocks.

That's part of the story, but it ends with David holding up the severed head of Goliath. For obvious reasons you won't see the image on a mural outside a preschool room.

Make no mistake about it. We're not in that picture. We're the Israelite soldiers, who wouldn't dare challenge Goliath on their own, cheering on from the sidelines.

Goliath is the picture of death and sin that we can't defeat. Jesus utterly destroys it for us. That's how you preach Christ in an Old Testament sermon. In church revitalization our people need to understand the role of Christ in their own regenerated heart and the role of Christ in reviving their church. They're linked together and essential for us to understand.

Moralistic tales that anyone in the theistic world can affirm won't revive a dying church. Instead, revitalizations are built on a clear gospel presentation where Christ is at the center of all things.

The Boundary of Contextual Deficiency in Preaching

When I was at Wornall, I prayed every week over the people who sat in the pews of the sanctuary. I thought about the challenges they faced and the limited theological understanding they might have. I knew as I prepared sermons that I had a diverse audience—from seminary students and retired pastors to atheists and agnostics.

When we preach, we're not just giving a lecture to show our biblical knowledge. We're connecting God's Word to the lives of the people we serve.

Honestly, I get worn out by pastors who spend fourteen hours a week on sermon prep and all of it is with their headphones on in a coffee shop. Sermon prep isn't just the time you spend with your Bible open, in a front of a computer screen, or in prayer. You're doing sermon prep when you visit members in their homes. You're doing sermon prep when you have breakfast with one of your members before work. You're doing sermon prep when you show up at the T-ball game and sit and talk with parents who attend your church. Whenever you're interacting with your congregants and you're learning about their lives, you're preparing to preach.

I listen to many great sermons, which are impeccably prepared, that aren't connecting to the lives of the people in the pews. Many churches decline because the pastor is preaching sermons that connected well to his congregation a decade ago, but the congregation isn't the same as it was a decade ago. Many of the members have gone on to heaven, they're in a senior care center, or they've moved away and they're not there every Sunday. The pastor hasn't changed his preaching.

Today you likely have people coming to your church whose worldviews are vastly different from the people you were preaching to a decade ago. You don't have to water down your preaching. You don't have to back off from the vitality of Scriptures. If anything, you need to be clearer about it because you're likely preaching to many people who don't know what you're talking about.

Let me give you an example. About eighteen years ago my wife and I were planting a church in Montreal, Quebec. The work was hard. People in Montreal are resistant to the gospel. When we arrived in Quebec, fewer than two out of one hundred people considered themselves evangelical Christians.

As we got started, a few people began to attend. One of those was a pastry chef from Lebanon. I often referred to other biblical passages when I preached by saying, "You know the Bible story of X." In one sermon I referenced the story of the prodigal son that way. That gentleman stood and said, "I don't know that story. I don't know any stories. Would you quit saying, 'I guess you know the story' and tell me the story?" And that's what I did. I needed to hear that. It forever reminded me of the importance of understanding my preaching context. You need to know the context of the people you're engaging. You need to understand what they know and what they don't.

I can't explain a lack of contextual preaching any better than that. I should have been aware that I had people in the congregation who didn't know most of the biblical stories. That's not watering down the Bible. It's communicating it effectively.

To preach contextually you need to get feedback, too. You might like to hear from the people who shake your hand when they leave and tell you what a wonderful job you did, but that feedback isn't helpful. Instead, gather some guys around you weekly to provide honest feedback on your sermons. The first time I did this, many of the people were reluctant to be open. Over time they became good at it. They'd let me know if I told too many stories, drifted from the Bible too much, or didn't connect to the audience.

Your preaching matters more than you know to your church revitalization efforts. Bible bingo, Christless preaching, and out-of-context preaching will sink your church's revitalization efforts. Make every effort to cross those barriers.

RUBICON 3: EVANGELISM

The Great Commission Code

In addressing the next two Rubicons, we wanted to provide a primer to the thought process. In recent years I have begun to develop my own illustrative imagery to assist pastors in understanding how the Great Commission connects both evangelism and discipleship. It is a DNA double helix. Think about it for a moment; picture the double helix. The *Collins English Dictionary* (2012) defines it this way: "the form of the molecular structure of DNA, consisting of two helical polynucleotide chains linked by hydrogen bonds and coiled around the same axis." "Coiled around the same axis" is our point. The axis is the Great Commission. The two helical polynucleotide chains are evangelism and discipleship. The links of hydrogen bonds are the key functions of what we do as the local body of believers.

Remember in 1993 when *Jurassic Park* was released? Dinosaurs were recreated by breaking down the DNA code from amber-encased mosquitos which had the blood of dinosaurs. Then using present-day reptiles, they attempted to repair the missing code. And of course pushing the evolutionary agenda, the movie goes on to show how evolution would not allow that decision to constrain dinosaurs being birthed naturally in the wild. The point of the illustration is focused on the DNA code. When pieces of the DNA were missing, they tried to use man-made methods to "fix" the problem. How often are we doing this in the church? If the Great Commission is the image of a double helix, when portions of our code do not exist, we try to force our methods to complete the code. This is not biblical. We have the code! The Great Commission code is locked in our mandate from Christ Himself. "Go . . . and make disciples, . . . teaching them." We must have a model and process for effective evangelism *and* discipleship if this is a Rubicon issue for your church.

The Great Commission Code is what binds together the church for gospel advance. Whether we look to the Great Commission itself in Matthew 28:19–20 or other verses throughout the Bible that provide for us this same mantra of the need to advance God's mission while we are on earth, one thing is perfectly clear: God desires to be in relationship with His people. Throughout the Old Testament we see this with the nation of Israel. With the coming of Jesus and His subsequent death on a cross, burial, resurrection, and ascension to the right hand of the Father radically shifting the old covenant and establishing the new covenant, we have our purpose.

In Deuteronomy 6 we see the calling of the father (establishing the gospel purpose for the family) to make God and His mighty works known to His children.

In Psalm 78:4 we again see the need to tell the coming generation the "glorious deeds of the LORD."

Acts 1:8 establishes the Great Commission with a missional strategy for the local church to consider. It challenges the church to ask, "Where is my Jerusalem? Judea? Samaria? And to what extent are the ends of the earth for this church?"

All of this intrinsically focused on one common word. We can sum it up with a term out of the ancient world, *kerygma*.

Kerygma

"The kerygma is essentially the same as the gospel, although the term itself emphasizes the manner of delivery somewhat more than the message that is being proclaimed. In the ancient world the king made known his decrees by means of a kerux (a town crier or herald). This person, who often served as a close confidant of the king, would travel throughout the realm announcing to the people whatever the king wished to make known. It is this note of authoritative declaration that is so appropriately transferred to the evangelizing activities of the primitive church."[8]

The idea of a herald proclaiming the gospel is a major revitalization method. One essential role of a pastor in revitalization is for *kerygma* to be accomplished. The message of Christ proclaimed to the community cultivates the environment for lostness to be impacted. As such, the pastor must determine he will not turn back where evangelism is concerned. As a reminder, *Rubicon* is the decision not to turn around but to press forward, the line in the sand, the point of no return—you must move forward. Where evangelism is concerned for a revitalization church, or any church, you cannot turn from it. The issue of evangelism is always the *how* question. How will we accomplish *kerygma* in our unique context?

So one might ask, Why is evangelism a Rubicon issue? I point to the church at Ephesus, Revelation 2:4 specifically. As we read verses 2–3, we see a great testimony any church would love to have said of them: "I know your works, your toil and your patient endurance, and how you cannot bear with those who are evil, but have tested those who call themselves apostles and are not, and found them to be false. I know you are enduring patiently and bearing up for my name's sake, and you have not grown weary."

What a testimony of the church. By all appearances they were doing what needs to be done. Standing for truth? Yes! Standing against false teachers? Yes! Continuing to serve faithfully? Yes! Then comes verse 4. This is the issue. Jesus Himself says: "I have this against you."

Wow. What a sudden turn. Can you imagine? What if you were a member of this church and you got the note from Jesus saying, "I have this against you." What would you think? "But Jesus, we are doing all these good things. How could You be disappointed? What else do You think we should be doing? Can't You tell we are not weary? I mean not yet, but if You want us to add one more thing, we might get weary. What could it be?"

I know, we have no idea what they were thinking. What a thought, if your church today got such a message from God. And this message is an easy fix, as it is the foundation of why the church exists. Make Jesus known. "I have this against you." What a powerful thought. Specifically, they had lost their first love. *Kerygma!* The passion they once had to share the gospel. They had become so busy with "important" things for the church to do that they had forgotten the most important thing.

Is this your church? Could this letter be written about your congregation?

Today's church can learn from the warning to Ephesus regarding the failure of evangelism. Many comparisons could be made in Southern Baptist life to the reality we find in Ephesus. In Southern Baptist life we have seen a tireless work to remain faithful to the inerrancy of God's Word through the conservative resurgence of the late seventies and into the nineties. However, during this same time we have seen baptisms decline. Our local churches remain faithful to standing for the Word of God; however, we are not standing faithful on our zeal of evangelism. We must not neglect our doctrinal position, but we must begin again with a true zeal for evangelism.

Yes, ministry needs to occur. We need to care for the widows and orphans. We need to teach new converts the truth of God's Word. We should gather to sing praises (whether hymns, southern gospel, contemporary, or some other God-honoring music). However, as soon as any of these important things overshadows the most important thing, we have positioned ourselves to receive such a letter as this.

With this ever present in our minds, let's think through a few areas to address the need to make evangelism a Rubicon moment in the life of our churches.

Context Is Key

As we address context, let us begin with this simple thought. The pastor is responsible for being the cultural, exegetical expert on his community. Pastor, you should know your community better than anyone else.

In answering the *how* question, a pastor must consider his context. Some churches in more pioneer areas might not use door-to-door evangelism due to their context. Cities might have codes against open solicitation. Another issue is an area of your community with gated subdivisions. They have gates for a reason, and typically residents are not excited about open solicitation. Now, most areas have exceptions to this solicitation conversation. If you are following up on a guest to your church, who gave you contact information, then it is not solicitation. However, if you are simply knocking on doors, whether you are doing community surveys or placing door hangers on homes, those are technically considered solicitation. I believe we need to listen cautiously to Jesus's counsel on issues of the government. He states that He put civic leaders in place to rule. "Let every person be subject to the governing authorities. For there is no authority except from God, and those that exist have been instituted by God" (Rom. 13:1). Churches should follow the law of the land. You can still find ways to be evangelistic in these more "closed" communities.

First, gospel advance is about relationships. Therefore, our first goal should not be door-to-door evangelism (though there is nothing wrong with this) but, rather, relationship building. If we want to see lives changed, it will be through establishing relationships with persons in the community and then growing those relationships to a point where they allow us to share our faith story. Many communities today are not closed, but they function as if they are. We pull into our driveways, park in our garages, and use the inside door so we do not have to see our neighbors. The children stay inside playing video games and not interacting with other kids in the yard and community. We have created our own closed communities and use that as our excuse for not witnessing. We must transition from this mind-set into one of great passion for impacting lostness.

The Great Commission should be the believer's life mission statement. We have an imperative, "Go." As such, we must go out of our homes, out of our garages, into the community, and engage lostness as this is what Jesus intended for us to do. We are called to be on mission where we live. This is the further call from Acts 1.8: to be the witness of Jesus in Jerusalem—where you live. Then we are to expand our missional strategy into Judea, Samaria, until the ends of the earth have heard the good news. Gospel advance is about being intentional in your life and being on mission.

Second, door-to-door evangelism is not out-of-date. Another way of saying this is, it still works. Many, honestly most, communities today do not have issues with door-to-door solicitation. This is true in the South, in much of the North, and across the plains states as well. Yes, certain communities have issues, but overall this type of visitation still works. How do we know? Because we have fast-growing, rapidly reproducing churches who are doing it. Established churches and new church plants engage in door-to-door evangelism. Some areas are heavily inundated with cultic groups that use door-to-door methods. Due to this, evangelistic churches discover it may be difficult at times to overcome opinions of the community who presume they are alike. As such, you do have to consider your community context to implement door-to-door strategies. It still works!

Third, even if your community is closed, that is no excuse for not doing evangelism in the community (see first point). You will need to get creative. Use inviter events to accomplish this. These events should be contextualized for your community. One church I know of in a more rural setting had never hosted a men's dinner. With all the hunters and fishermen at the church, it was a no brainer: Wild Game Dinner. They set up exhibits for hunters and fishermen. They found a gentleman in the community who was learning the trade of blacksmithing and making his own black powder rifle. He was invited to set up a booth and work on his rifle while the boys and men (who were like boys for this exhibit) watched and discussed his handiwork with him. All while eating wild game.

The men of the church invited friends, and the church gave away large door prizes. To win you had to do two things—attend and give your contact information on the door prize card. The church even included a statement across the bottom: "By registering for door prizes, you are giving Anywhere Baptist Church permission to contact you via email,

mail, phone calls, or in person." They knew what they were doing. The men wanted the nice door prizes. The church wanted their contact information. This gave the church prospects for months.

My final point on this issue is simple: if evangelism is a Rubicon for your church, you will discover ways to make Jesus known. Evangelistic endeavors become a lens from which each decision is made. You will begin to ask the question of gospel impact with everything you do. In the life of the church, this focus is remembering the first love of the church. This insures the church will not be accused with the same problem of the church of Ephesus and losing its first love.

Talk Is Cheap

Many churches like to talk about evangelism. As we work with churches in a state of plateau or decline, the conversation will always involve the evaluation of an evangelistic culture in the church. In over twenty years of consulting work, I have never had a church who stated they were not evangelistic. Many acknowledged they could do better, but none have said, "We simply are not evangelistic." However, when a church has not baptized anyone in three, four, or even ten years, they do not have to tell me they are not evangelistic. Rather, I typically have to tell them.

Oftentimes I will hear a pastor quote Isaiah 55:11a, noting that God's Word will not return empty or void in reference to their preaching. The rest of the passage is just as powerful: "But it shall accomplish that which I purpose, and shall succeed in the thing for which I sent it." God became flesh in the form of Jesus. Jesus is the Word, John 1:1. The purpose of Jesus's coming, the purpose of the Bible, is *kerygma*. Gospel advance. Evangelism. Isaiah 55:11 tells us the reason God's Word will not return empty is because He has a purpose and sent Jesus for a reason. The reason is to establish a radical shift in how God will relate to His creation. At the ascension of Jesus and the sending of the Spirit, God was saying the gospel is now open to the world. As such, the Great Commission is the motivating factor for all we say and do. We have a responsibility not just to say we are evangelistic, but rather to be evangelistic.

We must move beyond talking about evangelism and move toward telling others about Jesus. We can no longer say evangelism is a core value of our congregation and be satisfied with zero baptisms or professions of faith. If we are going to engage in programs that are supposedly evangelistic, we need to evaluate their effectiveness to see if they are actually reaching people for Jesus. We should "go into all the world" for the cause of making Jesus known.

Action Is Necessary

Let's end where we began. Deuteronomy 6, the Shema, is a call to action for the family. The real action item is found in verse 7, "You shall teach them diligently to your children, and shall talk of them when you sit in your house, and when you walk by the way, and when you lie down, and when you rise." The issue for Israel was covenant, and the same is true for Christians today. We are a covenant people, established by the blood of Christ Himself. Therefore, we are supposed to instruct with great diligence, in all of life that we live, the covenant relationship we have with Jesus.

Continuing with the concept from Psalm 78, this is making God and His glorious wonders known. We have a part in the grand story of God. He has chosen to work through us in proclaiming His truths to a lost and dying world. Our actions demonstrate our true core values. If we are going to say we are evangelistic as a church, we must tell the redemptive story of Jesus and issue an invitation for all we come in contact with to receive Jesus as Lord and Savior.

Matthew 28:19–20 and Acts 1:8 are our missional mandate for revitalizing a church. The Great Commission provides what I see as a simple answer to turning a church around. Lead someone to Jesus. This is not complex. Once you reach someone for Jesus, reach someone else.

In "Rubicon 4: Discipleship" we will provide the balance to the Great Commission that oftentimes is overlooked. But for the Rubicon of evangelism, let it serve as a reminder to wade into the waters with a mind-set of not turning back. We must once again walk down the path of reaching people for Jesus. Millions of lost people across North America and billions around the world need Jesus. To accomplish this we need to put action to our beliefs. The Great Commission is not about Christians talking in our holy huddles about evangelism. Rather it is about Christians being on mission in their respective communities with the gospel. *Kerygma!*

RUBICON 4: DISCIPLESHIP

Continuing with my double helix illustration for the purpose of discipleship, the hydrogen bonds represent key functions of what we do as believers. This includes Romans 12:1–2 as part of this bonding of evangelism and discipleship together in the Great Commission Code. I see this passage as outlining our calling for discipleship. Let's break down these bonds.

Bond 1: "Present Your Bodies as a Living Sacrifice"

Our first bond is an action on our part as believers. This action is considered spiritual worship. So, what does it mean to present oneself as a living sacrifice? Essentially, this is a complete and total commitment to God. We are to make ourselves available for God to use as He sees appropriate. He created us with personal desires and preferences. However, in making yourself a sacrifice to God, you are saying, "I am here to be used even if it is outside my preferences."

I once served with a pastor who shared with me he was timid to stand in front of the congregation. He had massive anxiety about preaching every week. However, because it was what God had called him to do, he walked through the anxiety and presented himself as a living sacrifice as he preached God's Word faithfully—and honestly was a gifted communicator in the midst of the anxiety. There are numerous similar stories, whether in ministry vocationally or some other profession. Making ourselves available for God to use in His timing and His ways is the total commitment He is seeking in us.

Bond 2: "Holy and Acceptable"

Being holy by definition is being spiritually excellent. One of my mentors, Dillard Wilbanks, always encouraged me to strive for perfection and settle for excellence. Being spiritually excellent is a lofty goal. However, because of Christ living in us, it is attainable, in a sense. This call to holiness is to live a Christlike life. To live this way, we might reflect back to the Christian swag of the 1990s and ask the WWJD question: *What would Jesus do?* In every decision we make, we should be seeking the counsel of Jesus, determining how He would respond and react to life's circumstances.

If we study His Word, we become acclimated to how He would respond. Studying His Word must be part of the discipleship process. There has been a movement away from university-modeled discipleship classes—the whole 101, 201, etc.; Foundations of the Faith: Survival Kit; *MasterLife* types of courses. We hear talk today of how Jesus "lived life" with His disciples; therefore, discipleship is supposed to be "living life" together. I get the well-intended comment. Here is my issue: we are doing a disservice when we overemphasize "living life" together and ignore the times when Jesus actually held class. Let's look at an example of this, which is not isolated throughout the Gospels.

In Matthew 10, Jesus is instructing, discipling, His disciples before sending them out to teach on the kingdom of God. This is not the living life together of discipleship, but the specific instruction of what His followers were to do. Look at the story of the rich young ruler in Mark 10:17–31. We have a teaching in the presence of others as the young ruler asks and is answered about what he should do to receive eternal life. After Jesus answers the young man, he turns to His disciples to teach/instruct/disciple them about the kingdom.

These are just a couple of illustrations throughout the Gospels. My point: discipleship is more than simply living life together. It is also specific instruction and knowledge about the Word of God. We must not allow our churches to drift from instructing in the Scriptures through discipleship class models simply because a group of persons got together to decide for all that discipleship occurs through living live together. What all of us should be saying is both/and, not one over the other. This is what Jesus did.

All I am saying with this illustration is Bible knowledge, which is gleaned from university-modeled discipleship classes, needs to be a part of everyone's holistic discipleship strategy. An adage says, "Practice makes perfect." A colleague pointed out to me one time, this is actually not true. Practice makes permanent. If you are practicing swinging the golf club wrong, you will get to the tee box and swing wrong because you have practiced and are now in the habit of doing it wrong. We do not need to rely on "living life" together without a measurement of who is spiritually excellent.

A small group leader could be practicing discipleship wrong and, therefore, leading others down a wrong path. Whereas, if we refer to the Master Teacher Himself, then we have the markers for spiritual excellence in which to strive. This means attending discipleship classes where we study the Word of God will give us an idea of how we can live life together.

Look at the Sunday school/small group ministry. This group should be the origination point of discipleship. This is where Bible teaching begins, and then from here we should live life together as an outward flow of our faith community. This is where the knowledge of Bible learning begins, in the small group faith community. In this community the leaders can address key doctrinal needs and demonstrate how the Word of God relates to the life of believers and is just as relevant today as when it was originally penned.

How can we be found acceptable to God but by his Holy Spirit indwelling in us? Both the words *holy* and *acceptable* are descriptors of what type of sacrifice we should be. Therefore, our discipleship strategy must be focused on leading persons into what is deemed by God as an acceptable lifestyle. Think about what an acceptable sacrifice was in the Old Testament. Clean. Without blemish. Remember Cain and Abel? "But for Cain and his offering he [God] had no regard. So Cain was very angry, and his face fell. The LORD said to Cain, 'Why are you angry, and why has your face fallen? If you do well, will you not be accepted? And if you do not do well, sin is crouching at the door. Its desire is contrary to you, but you must rule over it'" (Gen. 4:5–7).

The word "accepted" here in the Hebrew refers to the lifting up of one's face. We can take from this passage an acceptable sacrifice is one that encourages us to stand before God having done well. Connotations of Matthew 25:23 come to mind, "Well done, good and faithful servant." Being acceptable before God means as believers we are participating in the spiritual practices, which leads to transforming into the image of Christ. Much has been written on spiritual practices (or disciplines) so I will not spend time on such here, but the encouragement is to live in such a way to lift up your face before God.

Bond 3: "Do Not Be Conformed"

To be conformed is to mold your behavior into a set pattern or a set of standards. The encouragement in the text for the disciple is, do not have the same set of standards the world uses. Doing so is setting a faithfulness toward things that are not of God. We are to turn from these things and not be found leading a lifestyle that would cause us to drift from the holy and acceptable sacrifice we claim as we present ourselves. Our worldview must be focused on the things of God. The next phrase begins telling us how to do this.

Bond 4: Be Transformed by the Renewal of Your Mind

The Greek word for "transformed" is *metamorphoo*. This word means "to change form," as in the English derivative "metamorphosis," in addition to meaning "transfigure" in Matthew 17:2. In Paul's letters, this word is used to describe an inward, metabolic-like renewal of a Christian's mind through which an inner spirit is changed into the likeness of Christ. Paul told the Romans believers: "Do not be conformed to this world; but be transformed by the renewing of your mind" (Rom. 12:2, NASB). The best way to escape conforming to this world is not by trying to be unlike the world, but by allowing ourselves to become like Christ. Furthermore, this change is not effected by a change in outward behavior, but by a change in one's thinking. Transformation begins in the mind and continues in the mind. A transformed mind produces transformed behavior.[9]

Bond 5: Testing You

To be tested, in this meaning, has to do with authenticity. God is seeking genuine followers, true disciples, those who are authentic in their faith. Much today is said about authenticity. We hear how millennials are seeking authentic relationships. We are told they are looking for authentic leaders in all aspects of life, but especially church. My only question is, Hasn't this always been the case? I am a GenXer, and I have always sought authenticity in relationships and leaders. I presume my parents did as well since apparently I was reared to be this way.

We spend too much time trying to attribute characteristics based on generations instead of focusing on what Scripture teaches. If God is testing us for authenticity, then He has placed within out spiritual core this desire to strive for such a spiritual journey. This is not a generational identifier; this is a biblical quality. This is the life of a disciple. Be true. Be real. Be authentic about Christ.

Bond 7: "Discern ... the Will of God"

I believe this is the hardest part of being a disciple. How can we really know the will of God in our lives? Where does this ability of discernment come from? Let's travel back up the bonds within our Great Commission Code of the DNA and remember, it is because the Holy Spirit dwells in us. The Spirit gives us the ability to discern the will of God in our lives. However, sometimes we are over-spiritualizing life. We sit and pray waiting for an answer from God, wanting Him to give us the green light to move forward, all the while we miss the Great Commission moment by having our face down. Remember, if we are holy and acceptable as a living sacrifice, then our face will be lifted up. In the upright position we see what God is doing; we see the Great Commission moment. With our face lifted up, we see how God is presently working.

Someone in our circle of influence needs Jesus, and we pray—and we should pray. However, if all we do is pray, we will never introduce that person to Christ. We pray for the right moment. We pray our friend's heart will be receptive. We pray we will have the courage. But we never go up and speak.

The will of God is to make Jesus known in this world. The will of God for the disciple is to be the vessel God uses in making Jesus known. If you are a living sacrifice before God, take action. Move forward. God does not always say yes when we make a request of Him. Sometimes the answer we should be seeking is "God, is this a no moment?" And if He does not say no, then we move forward until He does. Too often disciples are looking for God's yes as the stamp of approval. When the harvest is plenty, the laborers are few, if God does not say no as happened to Paul when wanting to go to Bythinia, then lift your face and seek Great Commission moments.

Bond 8: "Good and Acceptable and Perfect"

We return to "acceptable," but now we have two additional words with it: "good" and "perfect." The word *good* refers to qualities that are generally moral and agreeable. Christian goodness means "honorable or noble characteristics." Therefore, a disciple demonstrates characteristics associated with being honorable. God accepts your lifestyle and finds it pleasing to Him. When we add the word *perfect*, we then have the complete or whole, meaning without blemish. Again this goes back to the earlier charge to live sacrificially.

Being complete or whole may also refer to one's integrity. Therefore, being good, acceptable, and perfect describes a disciple who has a lifestyle of integrity and honor before the Lord.

Conclusion

Wrapping up this section on the Great Commission Code demonstrates the Rubicons of evangelism and discipleship are not only important, but essential for every church. When thinking revitalization, they become the lifeblood for the kingdom work that needs to be accomplished. A strategy that permits the church to move forward in reaching the lost and discipling the new converts and maturing disciples requires intentionality. As such, the local church must engage the Great Commission Code and not neglect one strand of our double helix for the other. Doing so will cause the church to be off balance. A healthy church must have balance between these two Rubicon issues.

RUBICON 5: LEADERSHIP

The call to church leadership is challenging. The need for effective leadership in revitalization is necessary. The issue we often have in church revitalization is a leadership vacuum. What seems to occur are many high-capacity leaders leave the church during difficult times, which then sets the stage for continued loss of membership. A good rule of thumb for leadership ratios in a church is one leader for every eight members. As leaders vacate the church, the ratios increase, thereby causing undeveloped, or underdeveloped, laity to leave as well. Soon only a remnant is left. Certainly a few matriarch/patriarch types stand firm due to the heritage they have with the church, but many effective leaders are gone. A revitalization pastor enters a bleak situation. His primary role as the new pastor is reach new people for Christ. Second is the call to develop new leaders. In the midst of turmoil and chaos, this becomes challenging.

The Rubicon of leadership requires a pastor first to determine he is going to be the leader of the church. This is an intentional decision each pastor must make for himself. In making this decision, you may have to address unhealthy models within the church such as a patriarch/matriarch issue or a group of deacons controlling the decisions of the church. The pastor is called of God and affirmed by the local congregation to serve as the undershepherd. This means positionally you are the leader. The question is, are you functioning as the leader and are the congregants following your leadership style.

Mike Smith, president of Jacksonville College in Florida, wrote a dissertation addressing leadership styles and conflict. As part of this, he did a sampling survey of more than a thousand pastors in Texas using the DISC profile system. He determined that a majority of pastors fall into an analytic category, the C in DISC. Let's refresh this profile.

- **D** is the dominant personality, outgoing and task focused.

- **I** is the inspiring personality, outgoing and people focused.

- **S** is the supportive personality, reserved yet people focused.

- **C** is the analytical personality, reserved and task focused.

Think about this for a moment: a majority of pastors are reserved and task focused. Yet the need in the revitalizing church is for pastors who are outgoing and task focused. This means most pastors will need to function in what is referred to as an adjusted personality type. Meaning, this is not at the core of who they are, but it is what the church need. Many successful revitalization pastors are naturally in this category. The challenge is for the established church pastor who would like to revitalize his existing church pastorate.

A word of caution about this personality type for the pastor who naturally is a high D: you can be a bulldozer. In fact, the animal imagery associated with this personality is that of a lion. The dominant personality can be overbearing. This is also why being a C personality can work well in revitalization. You learn to adopt the traits of the D personality and do not actually function at your core this way. As a reserved but task-focused person, you can weed through the tall grass of relationships and ensure you do not become overbearing, which could cause relationship issues within the church leading to conflict.

The type C personality needs to be intentional, though, in developing relationships and not simply sit in the office studying and analyzing. In fact, many of our churches are in a state of decline due to pastors who believe their job is to preach, and therefore they spend all of their time focused on study. Is this important? Yes! Certainly, it is a priority. This is your calling. Along with preaching, however, the pastor has a number of roles he must fulfill.

Several years ago in Texas, we launched a conference entitled The Role of the Pastor. Part of the response from pastors was, "Don't you mean roles? We do more than one thing." The idea is, you are one pastor, and therefore you have one role, and that is to be the pastor. Within that role you have a plethora of functions. Preaching is one of them. Others include evangelist, discipler, administrator, undershepherd, counselor, and the list goes on and includes leader.

After establishing the way God needs you to lead, focus on building organizational health. As the leader, this is your role. So, how do you establish the health in an organization? Assemble a revitalization team.

Our frame is that of Baptist polity, so we can speak into this more than others. As Southern Baptists, our churches are autonomous. There is no authority telling churches how to function aside from Scripture. As such, the local church is congregational. Yes, there are many expressions of congregationalism, from single elder, plurality of elders, committee structure, etc. Ultimately, the congregation decides its polity, and has the right to change the polity with a vote of the church to whichever structure they desire under their present leaders with a simple rewrite of the bylaws (which most likely needs to be done in a revitalization church).

At the core, we are congregational. As such, in church revitalization the most effective way to lead in this context is through a revitalization team. This lead team assists the pastor with decision making, recruiting leaders for needs-based leadership. This means addressing the immediate needs of the church and developing a plan for growing leaders as new needs arise. The goal is to assemble a group of committed, core church members who will engage with the pastor to accomplish the ministry of the church by advancing the gospel in their present context.

Let's face it, a lot of work needs to be done. We have previously established the most important work of the church is advancing the mission of the gospel. As such, leaders must be able to function on multiple levels.

The position of pastor is crucial to the effectiveness of a local church in revitalization. He is key to making disciples. We note a major shift after the ascension of Christ in spiritual leadership. Think about it—throughout the Old Testament the father of the home was charged with discipling the family. Look at Deuteronomy 6. We see priests conducting the spiritual sacraments and services of the day along with prophets empowered by the Spirit of God to proclaim God and His ways to a culture. However, in the New Testament we begin to see the apostles make the shift in strategy, establishing a model of elders of the church. Typically men who had been mentored and discipled and charged to pass on to others what they have learned and been taught. So they reproduced reproducible leaders.

This leads through the establishment of the New Testament church and fast-forwards to today, where we see the pastor-teacher as the primary leader of the church. We know God established qualifications for such leaders (1 Tim. 3:1–7). The witness of a pastor's life in a church and community is important for the effectiveness of the church. Additionally, Titus 1:5–9 provides the qualifications of the elder. Both passages provide around twenty-three spiritual traits elders/pastors should possess. Fifteen of the traits are duplicated. These can be outlined in four categories:

1. Inner character

2. Family directives

3. Prohibitive directives

4. Ministry requirements

We say all of this to highlight the importance of the pastor-teacher. And if his role is that important, then his message must be. The senior pastor must do several things as the leader. First, he must prepare to preach. Solid sermon preparation should take a minimum of fifteen hours, but upwards of twenty hours. Therefore, half of a pastor's regularly scheduled hours are given to sermon preparation. Take another five hours for actual preaching and teaching times during the week, and over two-thirds of your hours are gone.

We have all heard Einstein's definition of insanity *ad nauseam*, but it is true. If we keep doing church the way we have been, we will continue to experience decline in many churches. LifeWay Research statistics tell us 29.9 percent of Southern Baptist churches are in decline and another 44.3 percent are plateaued. This means around 25.8 percent of churches in the Southern Baptist Convention are growing. I know some will argue these stats based on Annual Church Profile reporting, or lack thereof, but whatever the number, this is close. As such, only one-quarter of our churches are doing well. We have a problem.

So, how do you spend the other one-third of your time as a pastor? First, get past the thought of working only forty hours. Also, overcome your mindset of being on call 24–7. You need down time, and not every phone call is a crisis you must address. Train your leadership team to help you manage the ministry of the church. With two-thirds of your time gone, you have got to focus on reaching people for Jesus. Therefore, a commitment to several hours every week on evangelism is necessary. Let me encourage you with a resource at this point:

Mobilize to Evangelize by Matt Queen released in 2018 from Seminary Hill Press. Buy it. Use it.

Next, the senior pastor must commit time to developing his leadership team to address what the present greatest need is. Your time as the undershepherd of the church should be spent developing each leader to address specific needs. Determine which individuals have the greatest gift and calling to assist in these areas and develop them for each cause. Experientially, we can say what we typically see as the greatest needs after preaching and evangelism include discipleship, pastoral care (train up your deacons using a resource developed by Tony Wolfe, *A Deacon on Purpose: Four Biblical Essentials*, which can be purchased through sbtexas.com), and Bible teachers. Are there other needs? Yes, but these typically are the greatest needs we discover in revitalization.

A third area is persistent personal and professional development. Pastors will only be able to lead the members of their congregations to grow when they have been down the path themselves. Your personal development might include reading books, listening to podcasts, and attending conferences. The question a pastor always asks is, Which of these should I be using. Everyone has an opinion, and we will share ours here. Each year a pastor should read three or four books on preaching and communication. One of my favorite books to recommend pastors is *Crucial Conversations* by Kerry Patterson and Joseph Grenny. We have the most important conversation necessary for every person we encounter. Therefore, it is the most crucial. (As a side note, the complementing work called *Crucial Confrontations* is just as important for pastors, especially in a revitalization context, as there will be conflict. Knowing how to navigate these conflicts in a healthy organization is highly important.)

One of my mentors, the late Harry Piland, taught his philosphy in seminary: every pastor should be the theologian-in-residence at his church. This tells me pastors should also read books on theological and cultural issues. Therefore, reading two or three books a year on this subject would be beneficial. Other books to read fall into the categories of the needs of your church: evangelism, disciple-making, revitalization (after all, you are trying to turn the church around), and other relevant topics for the present need of your church.

The same could be said of conferences to attend. I recommend attending a preaching workshop offered by a seminary at least one time per year. The great model of these workshops is preparing you to preach expositionally through a book of the Bible. Currently, you may not be preparing to preach through that book during that particular year, but it could be future preparation for how God may direct your sermons over the next several years. Either way, you are getting solid preaching preparation by attending such a conference. Since two-thirds of your role as pastor is sermon preparation/presentation, attending one conference a year is vital. (A side note for church leaders reading this book: provide a path for your pastor to attend conferences. Give him a budget and conference days so he does not have to use vacation time. Conferences should be considered workdays, not time off).

Other conferences might be beneficial as well. Whether attending an evangelism conference, revitalization conference, or some other conference addressing the needs of the church, pastors should be continually develop themselves.

Another way is by networking with other pastors. A pastor/leader should be the cultural exegetical expert in his community. The only way to be this person is, first, to be in the community and, second, to engage with other pastors in the community to converse about the spiritual condition of your region. Ministry in isolation is not what God intended. We should engage with others to see/hear what they are experiencing and to share what you are experiencing. Oftentimes you will learn that though you thought you were the only one having certain issues, you are not.

In closing out the Rubicon of leadership, the pastor must decide to be the leader. He must be humble in function, but decisive in action. In revitalizing a church, work needs to be done, and the pastor must be the one leading the way. The pastor must communicate a fresh vision from God contextualized for the current congregation, demonstrating how the church can once again impact lostness in the community. A pastor focused on leading the church well can know his congregants will follow him. A pastor leading his church to reach the community can know the church will experience revitalization. A pastor who prepares himself in the role of a pastor can know with certainty that he is honoring the calling God has on his life and be able to echo the words of Paul: "I thank him who has given me strength, Christ Jesus our Lord, because he judged me faithful, appointing me to his service" (1 Tim. 1:12).

RUBICON 6: PROGRAMS

If you're over the age of fifty and grew up in the church, you probably remember a time when programs were like gold in the church. They always seemed to work. Whether it was a youth program, a children's program, a Bible study program, a missions education program, or a choir program, all you had to do was plug them into your church and they'd thrive.

That's how it was during most of my father's ministry. Throughout the 1950's, 1960's, and 1970's, churches in my Southern Baptist denomination grew like never before. Programs were the fuel that helped those churches grow. Southern Baptists had a program for everything and everyone. And those programs worked.

While the programs were effective, churches grew during that time because of whom the programs engaged. As churches reached out to young families led by the Builder Generation, programs resonated. This generation grew up in the Great Depression, came of age during World War II, and returned home to jobs at General Motors, AT&T, and TWA. They worked their entire lives for these companies.

When it came time to come to church, they flourished in the routine of programs. They awaited the January Bible Study. They joined Sunday school classes. They put their children in Royal Ambassadors and Girls in Action. Church choirs flourished.

Those programs worked until they didn't. My dad was an excellent pastor for more than fifty years. But one day my dad told me, "I don't think I could have pastored today." I knew what a good pastor he had been. I knew he could have done it.

"In all of my years in ministry, I never sat in my office for one hour and asked myself this basic question, 'How do I do church?'" he explained. "There was a program for everything we did. There was a Sunday school program. There was a youth program. There was a children's missions program. There was a Sunday night discipleship program. There was a visitation program. There was a January Bible Study. In many ways I wouldn't know how to get started without those programs."

That sums up the frustrations of many declining churches. The programs worked well in the past, but now they don't. Programs have become one of the most significant Rubicons in declining churches around the country.

If you want to see your church begin to make disciples that make disciples again, you'll have to cross the Rubicon of programs. Let me be clear though. Programs aren't all bad. In fact, sometimes programs will help you cross boundaries instead of blocking them. If we're not careful, they will block our revitalization efforts. Consider these three specific ways programs become Rubicons and limit meaningful revitalization.

Programs Validate Our Efforts

Even dysfunctional programs make us feel as if we're being effective and trying. The more we rely on these programs, the more they tend to validate our work. This is a false sense of validation.

You see, programs shouldn't validate what we do. We must find validation in what Jesus has done for us rather than what we're doing for Him.

When programs work, we feel like we're doing something. They give us a sense of worth. Our churches may still decline. The church may not have baptized anyone in two years. We may have no impact on the surrounding neighborhood. We still have our programs. They still "work," whatever that means. So, we don't need to make any other changes.

Dying churches tend to anesthetize the pain of death with an abundance of activity. I can't count the number of dying churches I've visited who don't think they're dying because they're still having meetings. People are still showing up. They're still conducting programs. But you look around the neighborhood, and no one is remotely impacted by those programs. The church isn't discipling any young believers. Despite all of that, the church feels validated because their programs are still running and doing what's expected.

It's a boundary we must cross if we want God to bring new life to our churches. If we let programs validate our ministries, they will kill our ministries.

Programs Give Us Our Value

Do you want to know how much programs mean to the people in your church? Try taking them away. Do that and you'll see just how much those programs mean to people. I've been involved a number of times in transitional church settings where I try to weed out unproductive programs. Invariably someone will come to my office in tears saying, "You don't understand. I need to do this. This brings me fulfillment. Running this program gives me a purpose."

That's a problem! For some people in our churches, their entire value comes from these programs. That's unhealthy for the person. That's unhealthy for the church. Our value doesn't come from a program we run. It comes from Jesus.

When individuals or churches find their value in programs, those programs become barriers to revitalization. It's really about trust. We can only place our trust in *either* programs or the Holy Spirit—never both.

Frankly, we love the control. When we place our trust in programs, we get a false sense of control of our situation. We can manage a program; we can't manage the Holy Spirit. That's why we place trust in the program in the first place. The more trust we place in the program, the less trust we have in Jesus.

Maybe you're asking, "Can't Jesus be in the program?" If He's in the program, that's great. Usually, He's not. The program tends to be about us, our work and our effort. *It's about our agenda for our church.* Jesus wants to lead us moment by moment into a new life for our churches, and we want to put in a program that'll help us control what happens over the next few years.

It's easier to trust a program than to take the risks necessary to follow Jesus. Henry Blackaby says so wonderfully, "God is under no obligation to resource your plans for His church, but He'll spare nothing from heaven to resource His plan for His church."

Programs aren't flexible. We can't pivot to follow Jesus into the next step because we're running a program that gets in the way. Jesus has a plan for every church. We must let go of our programs so we can take a hold of His plans for our churches. A revitalized church won't happen otherwise.

In many ways it is easier to trust in a program than to take risks and trust in Jesus for the next step in your church's journey. It's easier because the adversary doesn't want us to trust in Jesus. The adversary would rather we trust our own programs, our own abilities, and our own work than to trust in Jesus. He knows that the end result of trusting your programs over Jesus is death. Make no mistake about it. The adversary wants your church to die. He'll do whatever it takes—even getting you hooked on church program after church program—to see your church die.

Programs Vindicate Our Work

For true revitalization to happen in your church, you must—as the Bible describes in Revelation 2—remember how far you've fallen, repent, and return to what you did at first. Your church can't find new life until you do those three things.

Programs will stunt that process. As long as we focus on programs, we'll find it tough to repent and return. And it will especially be tough to repent. We'll blame our lack of success on bad programs and refuse to see what God wants us to see from those failures.

As I visit with declining churches, I often ask them what they believe is missing in the church. They'll usually say something like this: "We need a youth program. We used to have a big youth program that did great things in the community."

That's the last thing a declining church needs. A dying church needs the remaining people—even if it's just ten—to fall in love with the teenagers in the neighborhood. You need the remaining people to care deeply about teenagers who don't talk, walk, or look like them—and do not know Jesus.

Until those remaining members stop judging those teenagers and start loving them, no youth group will change the situation. Too often churches think if they can just get someone to run a youth program, they can sit back and see if the program works. If it doesn't work, they can say, "Well, we tried. It's not our fault."

Plugging in a youth program to that will just vindicate the church of its lack of love. It relieves them of responsibility. Here's the problem. Without repentance you won't have revitalization. The vindication we feel prevents us from remembering, repenting, and returning. Why should we do any of that? Our problems aren't our fault, we mistakenly believe. We just had a bad program.

We can't find our validation in programs. We can't place more value in programs than the Holy Spirit's leadership. We can't find our vindication in programs. I think sometimes, as a declining church, we just need to quit everything except prayer. Imagine if we just went three months and didn't have any programs at all. We simply cleaned out everything. We seek God's face and boldly tell Him, "We'll do whatever you want. We'll let go of every program that doesn't either make disciples who make disciples or make the community noticeably better for the glory of God. Nothing else matters."

If your church's programs aren't making disciples that make disciples, they're a barrier to revitalization. Think of it like this. Programs can serve as bridges, a structure that can get you across a barrier. It's temporary, something you use because God asked you to do so.

If you're not careful, that same structure that once helped you cross a barrier will become a wall. It will block your view of God instead of helping you along His path.

You don't want any part in that. Your church doesn't want any part of that. Take a long look at the programs in your church. If a program doesn't help you make disciples who make disciples, dump it. The program isn't worth it.

RUBICON 7: POLITY

Your greatest challenge to revitalize your church may not come from your preaching, your building, or even your prayer life. It may be your own church polity. The very vehicle you've put in place to help you make decisions to move your church toward your mission may be pulling you away from it.

Your church's governance may torpedo your revitalization before you even start. I've worked with hundreds of dying churches across North America. I can tell you with absolute certainty that polity is one of the primary Rubicons we have to cross in order to revitalize our churches. Most churches at the end of their lives have completely convoluted polities. Their polities don't reflect who Jesus is or what the church is all about.

Often churches in this situation have a complete hodgepodge of different kinds of church governing structures that they've fastened together through many years of operation. Rather than just cleaning their polity out and starting from scratch, churches just keep adding different pieces. When a problem comes up, the church doesn't fix it with redemptive church discipline. They just keep adding different bylaws and governance to fix it. Eventually the polity becomes encumbered and turns into a barrier for any revitalization attempt.

The New Testament is clear about church polity. The church has a chief pastor, and we don't elect Him. A search committee doesn't find Him. Jesus Christ is the head and senior pastor of every church. He builds His church any way He'd like. He does it for its function, His glory, and our joy. All biblical church polity starts with this: *Jesus is the head of the church.* Yes, our churches will have pastors or elders (whichever term you use), but primarily the church is a place where Jesus is the head and the church selects godly men to be their pastors.

This is also important. Every time you read about a church in the New Testament, it's always described within the context of a plurality of leaders. The idea of one senior pastor who calls all the shots and hires some staff to help him do his work isn't from the Bible. Unfortunately, that's been a highly replicated model in my Southern Baptist background.

In many situations you also have deacons who almost serve as a church council on steroids. Sometimes the pastor even reports to them. You won't find that model in the Bible either.

As a lifelong Southern Baptist, I believe in congregational polity. At Wornall we had two groups of leaders—pastoral leaders and servant leaders. Both groups were elected by the congregation. I believe the Bible teaches that the congregation selects from among themselves men to lead the church. Often our polity doesn't reflect any of that. We govern ourselves through a hodgepodge of different approaches, and it greatly hinders us as we revitalize our churches.

Want to know whether your church needs to cross the polity Rubicon? Here are four clues.

Our Polity Reflects Our Preferences

Our goal should be for our churches to make disciples who make disciples and to leave a lasting impact on our community. Our polity should reflect those goals. The New Testament is our blueprint for how the church operates. Neither are often paramount in our polities. Rather, our preferences often lead the way.

We want monthly business meetings, so we stay updated on what's going on, in an effort to be "in the know." We build a polity based on what we've done before, what our church did when we were growing up, or what some book told us to do. Worse yet, we mix and match from several spots. We hear of a problem that happened at another church, so we make sure it won't happen in ours. At the end of the day, our polity is just our preferences.

After a while, our polity becomes a known, safe entity. We don't have to think about it. We don't have to study it. We don't have to question it. We revert to what we know. And, in the process, our polity limits our revitalization.

What's the alternative? Stop battling for preferences, and let Jesus be the chief pastor of our church—not just in empty words, but in full practice.

Our Polity Protects Power Brokers

Our polity becomes an obstacle to revitalization when it protects the church's "power brokers." Your church's power broker (or, at times, power brokers) may not be a deacon, an elder, or someone with a specific position in the church. Because of how your church set up the polity, this person or this family runs everything.

Your church may do its business meeting in a certain way, so this person keeps his or her power. Maybe everything has to be run through several layers of leadership, so this person has the time necessary to influence the decision.

This issue may not be obvious at first. It's hard to see, especially for a new pastor. It's not written down anywhere. The pastor search committee won't clue you in, but you won't be there long before you'll see the writing on the wall. It's how the church does business meetings. It's how church councils are run. It's how you select leaders. Whatever decision your church makes, whether it's big or small, this power broker's fingerprints are all over it.

When this happens, you don't have the option of changing your polity so it's better aligned with where Jesus wants to take your church. You can't change your polity, or you'll limit the authority of your power broker.

Can you see the problems here? A church God uses to make disciples who make disciples and transform the neighborhood for His glory has room for only one power broker—Jesus. You can't break through the boundary of polity until He is the only power broker who matters in your church.

Our Polity Exposes a Lack of Trust

One time my local director of missions and I were with a church that was down to a dozen people. They had lost their pastor, and we were meeting with the pastoral search committee. I wanted to encourage them to release their church and the remaining members to an outside entity so we could do a replant, but they didn't want to do that. They still had some money in the bank and could pay a pastor. And that's what they wanted to do.

The director of missions asked the search committee whether they had enough money to pay a full-time pastor or they planned to hire a part-time pastor. The chairman said the church didn't know yet. They had enough money to pay a full-time pastor for two years or a part-time pastor for four years.

The director of missions explained that we couldn't really help them find a candidate until we knew whether the pastor would be full-time or part-time. He suggested we talk about that issue before delving into anything else.

"No, that's not our decision," he told us. "That's up to the finance committee." The church had about ten to twelve people on most Sunday mornings. Five of them were sitting in that room. When I asked who was on the finance team, all of them raised their hands. "Who else is on the team?" I asked. Nobody, I was told.

"Can't we just talk as the finance team about whether you want to pay a part-time or full-time pastor?" the director of missions asked.

"We can't meet as the finance team right now," the chairman responded.

That's a polity that displays a remarkable lack of trust. Somewhere along the line, an individual or several individuals abused the leadership they were given. The church added a rule to make sure it never happened again.

These rules make it difficult for a church to make a good decision. The polity is no longer in place to make a better decision or help the church run smoother. In this case it was there to do the opposite. The rule was in place specifically to slow down the process. For the finance team to meet, they had to let everyone know so if anyone wanted to attend, they could. At first glance it probably seemed like this policy ensured no one did anything nefarious behind closed doors. It really just demonstrated that the church was on life support. With a dozen people, the church was ready to close, but they didn't even trust the remaining members to make the right decisions. In all fairness I think that group we met with trusted one another, but the policy was written at a time when they didn't.

You can't revitalize a church when the church doesn't trust one another. Where there is no trust within a church, the fellowship is broken. The church isn't submitting to the lordship of Christ or in loving relationship to one another.

The moment people start pulling out the bylaws during a business meeting, your church is in trouble. That's what happens when trust is gone. Churches need governance, but at the end of the day, churches are governed by consensus. Churches are flocks and families. We elect leaders and trust them to lead us. If churches second-guess everything their leaders do and put policies in place to inhibit their leadership, it points to a lack of trust, and that will limit revitalization.

Our Polity Reveals Our
Desire to Lead

Polity creates a boundary in our church when it shows people our congregants don't want to be led. They don't want to be led in worship. They want to pick the songs, determine the length of the sermon, set up the church's governance, etc.

Christians need to be led. Gathered worship gives us an opportunity to let someone else lead worship, pick the songs, pick the Scripture, and speak into our lives. Our spiritual health requires it. More importantly, the health of our churches depends on it.

The same is true for church governance. For revitalization to happen, we need to schedule fewer meetings—committee meetings, business meetings, etc.—and to place more trust in the leaders we've elected to serve the church.

I can sum up this whole chapter with one sentence. One sign of a dying church is that they find more value in the process of decision than the outcome of decision.

Let's be clear. Your church's decision-making process isn't where you want to place your trust. It's faulty. It's likely the product of our own deficiencies and preferences rather than the will of the Father. Thanks to the polity of many of our churches, the most carnal member can derail just about anything on the agenda, and we can't do anything to stop him. Everyone's voice is equal. Everyone must be heard. Our polity must be right. (We've had it forever, so it must be OK, right?)

Typically, if dying churches were half as interested in obeying Jesus and His gospel, loving one another, caring for one another as they are in their bylaws, they wouldn't be dying.

You simply can't trust your bylaws and the Holy Spirit at the same time.

Bylaws provide our churches with security. We need them. I'm not suggesting you rip yours up. We can't live by faith, confront Satan, and storm the gates of hell without taking risks. The Christian faith has always been a risk-taking faith. God has always called us to go against the grain. If our focus is on preserving our polity and keeping our little rules instead of boldly following Jesus, we might as well forgo revitalization. It won't happen anyway.

This doesn't mean elected church leaders won't ever abuse their power and fail the church. They will. Your church governance should provide a way for loving, corrective church discipline to take place with both members and leaders. You can do that without your church polity reinforcing your congregation's preferences, power brokers, lack of trust, and desire to lead.

The boundaries I described in this chapter simply don't match up with the picture of the New Testament church where Jesus is the head. When we function under the authority of Jesus, we select leaders from among us. They're accountable directly to the Lord, and He will keep them accountable for how they shepherd the church.

We don't need to create rules and attach them to our bylaws to encumber the ministry of the church. In the midst of revitalization, God will present you with ministry opportunities you must be prepared to seize. He'll open up doors only He can open. I've seen too many times where convoluted polity and church governance structure have closed doors God has so clearly opened. Don't let that happen to your church.

RUBICON 8: FACILITIES

Leading church revitalization work for a state convention affords me many opportunities to see churches at various stages of decline. One continued issue I confront is facility deterioration. The stages of revitalization typically look something like this as it relates to facilities:

Year 1: Budget decline; at this point the church defers facility upkeep. The thought, We will be able to shampoo the carpet, put on a fresh coat of paint, or whatever next year.

Year 2: We can close down that section of the church; we do not use that many rooms anyway.

Year 3: We can use the nursery for storage; we haven't had any babies in years.

On the story goes with the continued deterioration of the building, and the church is never able to restore the facilities.

In the most severe cases, the church declines to a point of wanting someone else to take over the property, and there is more deferred maintenance on the building than is sustainable. Eventually the realization hits: it is better to close the building and walk away with no hope of restoration. This is why the Rubicon of facilities is a point of no return. You must not defer maintenance and upkeep of your property. Appropriate facility upkeep must be intentionally prepared for and addressed long before budget cuts.

Curb Appeal

Let's begin on the outside. There are a plethora of home improvement shows on television today thanks to HGTV, DIY, and other channels available *en masse* through various media options. Oftentimes, these shows will address the outside of the property at some point. The thought in real estate, the way something looks will attract buyers. Apply this idea to your church. What would draw a person in to your church in the first place? This is where I typically hear the pushback, "Christians shouldn't worry about those things. They should come to church because . . ."

Now this is where I have to set the record straight. The church does not exist to reach Christians. Your church is not here for the churched person. Will you reach some? Yes. Someone new to the community moves in and is looking for a church. Let's be honest, they still want to attend somewhere that shows life and vibrancy. Worn-down facilities show neither.

The people you are trying to reach are unbelievers. They are lost. They do not come to church. Unbelievers are spiritually seeking, and they have a standard of what they see and know and accept in society.

A home with nice curb appeal is something to consider buying. A restaurant with nice curb appeal is worth trying. (I understand the concept of a dive, but a dive typically has a line of people coming out the doors; therefore, it is worth trying. If your church had a line of people coming out the door, we would not be having this conversation.)

We need to address the look of our church from the outside. You do not have to pave the parking lot. You can spray new surface to give it a fresher look and then paint new lines. (A volunteer team can easily manage painting the stripes. Appropriate measurements can be found online along with the code and regulations for being ADA compliant in your area.) If you don't have a paved lot, then no problem. Keep the lawn mowed and the shrubs pruned.

Again, if you are addressing curb appeal on a budget, do away with flowering plants, which require constant watering. Also, don't substitute gravel parking for asphalt unless you are in an area where it rains a lot. Women in their heels, disabled, the elderly, all find mobility on gravel difficult. Avoid decisions which can cause difficulty for people entering the building.

Finally, volunteers can paint the building to save money as well. At some point in our Western culture we moved away from the "church cleanup," days which had everyone at the church on a Saturday to give the building a fresh look. Now we prefer to spend our tithes and offerings on paying people to do these things instead of volunteering and then using our tithes and offerings for missions and ministry as intended. In church revitalization, and other churches should consider this as well to be better stewards of their resources, we need to volunteer some man hours to restore the physical appearance of our campus.

A Look Inside

Now let's walk through the front doors of the church. One church I was assisting in revitalization used the nursery for storage. When I arrived on Sunday morning to preach, I noticed this immediately. The nursery room was immediately across the hall from the sanctuary entrance, which is a great locale for young guest parents already skittish about leaving their babies with strangers. As I addressed some of the noticeable facility issues, I asked why they were using the nursery for storage. Someone responded with the standard, "We don't have any babies in our church."

My follow-up is pretty standard as well. Using the parable of the steward as my model, I asked why God would bring young families to a church that is not prepared for babies? I was presenting a thought to the church: if you are prepared, maybe God will choose to bless you for your preparedness.

Do I believe this? Most definitely. Being prepared is more than just cleaning out the room. It also includes having someone present and ready to receive guests. The church leaders received this principle of stewardship well and immediately took action. They reported back to me three weeks later. They had cleaned out the nursery from storage, and two leaders were prepared the next Sunday after my visit.

The two women were present for three Sundays, ready if guests arrived. And that is when it happened! God brought guests to the church on that third Sunday . . . with a baby.

What a blessing, and how excited this church was to have experienced this. Do not take this wrong; it is not a formula. I am not saying God will automatically bring babies because you clean out the nursery and have people present. However, I am questioning why God would bring babies to your church IF you are not prepared for them. This is the stewardship principle. Some churches I work with are not in communities where babies are being born; therefore, there is not a real likelihood of guests with children even coming to the church. The illustration is used for the purpose of why your facilities are a Rubicon issue for the church. This same concept should cross over to other areas of church ministry as well.

Look over your facilities. Clean out rooms that can be used for Bible study, children's ministry, students, etc. Things can be stored in closets and storage rooms. Some things may need to be discarded. If you have had a practice of gathering up things and saving them for the future, there might not be a future, so get rid of things that are not pertinent for present ministry and prepare the space for people. Mop, vacuum, paint, clean the carpets and the pew cushions, and deep clean the restrooms. Get everything as clean as you possibly can.

Make a project sheet of what must be remodeled and/or replaced. Start with the most pressing areas of ministry. Typically in addition to restoring classrooms for people, the restrooms will need to be remodeled. These are often neglected even though they are frequently used on a weekly basis. You may not have the skilled labor in your church to handle this type of work; however, there are church construction teams who will do the work for free if you provide the supplies. Ask your denomination for some assistance in finding such teams as a resource to you. Then the church can buy the needed supplies, and a work crew will come in and do the labor.

One church I worked with in revitalization has used this model. The pastor led the church to clean up the campus to the best of their abilities and then made his master list of things that needed to be repaired or replaced. With his master list in hand, he recruited work teams for mission trips to his church which provided the necessary skilled labor to complete the tasks. Some teams even bought supplies for him as part of their missional gift to the church. He has spent three years slowly working as the church has funds; and even though they are in an old building, they have remodeled restrooms, a renovated sanctuary, and a refreshed fellowship hall. What a blessing!

Use the Facility

I assisted another church in revitalization that had an elementary school across the street. Each week, Monday through Friday, you could stand in the front parking lot of the church and watch the families with young children drive past the church, bringing the children to school and picking them up. And yet within the church there were no children. The curb appeal was pleasant for the church. The inside of the building in good shape, but they were not reaching families.

Sometimes your facility's appearance is not the problem, but rather your facility's use. The church had not engaged the community in using the campus to attract families on the property. Now first, as we discussed in the Rubicon of evangelism, our job is to go to the community and not focus on bringing the community to the church. However, when the community is right across the street, the church needs to do some things with the facilities to draw attention to the campus and let the community know you want to minister to them. There are a number of ways you can do this.

Make your facility available to be used. Many churches in decline do not have the funds to pay for cleaning the property as we discussed previously, and therefore they start turning inward instead of outward. They no longer allow the community to use the property, or they start charging hefty fees to use the building so they can recoup some cleaning expenses and usage fees.

As an administrator, I agree the church may need to charge some type of fee, but engaging the community means you want to allow the use of your property for the lowest possible fee. Meaning, if the school wants to use your property for a teachers meeting, maybe you can allow them to use it and then enlist volunteers to clean the building afterward (and maybe before if necessary) in order to not charge the school a cleaning fee. This is one way you can bless the community.

In the example of this church across the street from the school, a ministry outreach to teachers one morning a month is another way of getting them on campus. Set up in the parking lot a stand with coffee and muffins for teachers. Post this on your church sign, or handwrite signs and place them along the front of the street: "Free coffee and muffins for teachers." Allow teachers to drive through your parking lot and pick up the snack items and coffee on their way to park their car. This is a great way to use your facility, make the church known, and minister to teachers in your community who, by the way, have families and may need a church home.

The Rubicon of facilities is an image of the church in the community. Once we decide not to ignore the needs of our campus, we can develop a plan for progress, using our campus for the glory of God. This plan is how we can mitigate the deterioration of our campus and, with volunteer assistance, lessen our budget expenses on the upkeep. Your campus should reflect a church that cares about your "look," demonstrating a concern you have for representing Jesus well where He has planted your church.

EPILOGUE

Our final thoughts on Rubicons are central to the question of, "So what?" So, what do we do with this information about Rubicons? Or better yet, what should a pastor do with this information? We are both practitioners. We do not write for philosophical reasons. These Rubicons are not philosophical thoughts to ponder and consider. These Rubicons are real issues for the church in revitalization. The reality, there are many churches which need to address these Rubicons, if not, they will need to be revitalized in the future. There is a false thought today, that a church cannot be revived. It has been said, dead churches cannot live again. Unfortunately for the persons who believe this, they have not fully studied the resurrection of Jesus. The resurrection of Christ came about by the power of the Spirit. This same Spirit, which was given to all Christians on the day of Pentecost, is still present and in believers today. As such, the dead church can be revived by the power of the Spirit. The Spirit has resurrection power. The church should, and the pastor must, address the Rubicons which are confronting the ministry of gospel advance. As pastors you must step into the waters under the influence of the power of the Spirit of God to lead the church. The die is cast. Are you willing to step into the waters?

Rubicon Review

Rubicon 1: Prayer. The Rubicon of prayer is when prayer has become a demands or expectation list for God.

Rubicon 2: Preaching. The Rubicon of preaching is a lack of expositional, biblical preaching of the gospel contextualized for the church's community.

Rubicon 3: Evangelism. The Rubicon of evangelism is the failure of the church to reach people for Christ.

Rubicon 4: Discipleship. The Rubicon of discipleship is the failure of the church to mature believers in the faith.

Rubicon 5: Leadership. The Rubicon of leadership can develop in several ways, one of which is those presently in leadership failing to pass along leadership to the emerging generations

Rubicon 6: Programs. The Rubicon of programs is when more emphasis is placed on the programs of the church and their respective ministries than on gospel advance.

Rubicon 7: Polity. The Rubicon of polity is allowing structure to mandate function of the church instead of God's Word.

Rubicon 8: Facilities. The Rubicon of facilities diverts budget from maintenance needs on the property.

ABOUT THE AUTHORS

Mark Clifton is The Senior Director of Revitalization/Replanting at the North American Mission Board. God has used Mark to lead in the planting and replanting of more than a dozen churches across the United States and Canada. Mark is married to Jill and they have two sons, two daughters in law and two grandsons.

Kenneth Priest serves as the Director of Convention Strategies for the Southern Baptists of Texas Convention in Grapevine, TX, leading revitalization endeavors since 2008. He holds a Doctor of Educational Ministry degree with an emphasis in Church Revitalization from Midwestern Baptist Theological Seminary (MBTS), Kansas City, MO. He serves as an adjunct professor of church revitalization in the doctoral program with MBTS and an adjunct professor of evangelism and church growth with The Southern Baptist Theological Seminary, Louisville, KY. Kenneth is married to Debbi.

NOTES

[1] Merriam-Webster, s.v. Rubicon, accessed August 22, 2-18, https://www.merriam-webster.com/dictionary/Rubicon.

[2] Walter A. Elwell and Barry J. Beitzel, "Prayer," *Baker Encyclopedia of the Bible* (Grand Rapids, MI: Baker Book House, 1988), 1745.

[3] C. H. Dodd, *The Apostolic Preaching and Its Development*, (Hodder & Stoughton Ltd., 1936), 7

[4] R. H. Mounce, "Preaching," ed. D. R. W. Wood et al., *New Bible Dictionary* (Leicester, England; Downers Grove, IL: InterVarsity Press, 1996), 950.

[5] William J. Larkin Jr., "Evangelize, Evangelism," *Evangelical Dictionary of Biblical Theology*, Baker Reference Library (Grand Rapids: Baker Book House, 1996), 216.

[6] Chris Byrley, "Discipleship," ed. Douglas Mangum et al., *Lexham Theological Wordbook*, Lexham Bible Reference Series (Bellingham, WA: Lexham Press, 2014).

[7] Craig A. Smith, "Church Leadership," ed. Douglas Mangum et al., *Lexham Theological Wordbook*, Lexham Bible Reference Series (Bellingham, WA: Lexham Press, 2014).

[8] Walter A. Elwell and Barry J. Beitzel, "Kerygma," *Baker Encyclopedia of the Bible* (Grand Rapids, MI: Baker Book House, 1988), 1261.

[9] Eugene E. Carpenter and Philip W. Comfort, *Holman Treasury of Key Bible Words: 200 Greek and 200 Hebrew Words Defined and Explained* (Nashville, TN: Broadman & Holman Publishers, 2000), 408.

Get the resource which is empowering a movement of church revitalization.

"Mark Hallock is one of the most important voices in this unprecedented need in the modern day to revitalize dying churches. *Replant Roadmap* is sure to become the practical how-to guide to lead this next generation into this noble work."

Brian Croft, Senior Pastor, Auburndale Baptist Church; Senior Fellow, Church Revitalization Center, The Southern Baptist Theological Seminary

REPLANT
roadmap

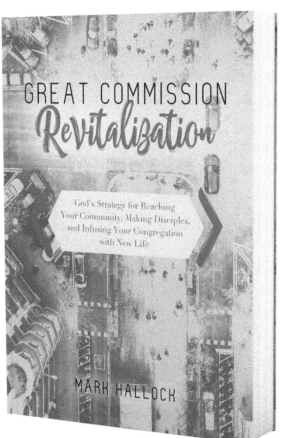

ACOMA PRESS

Acoma Press exists to make Jesus non-ignorable by equipping and encouraging churches through gospel-centered resources.

Toward this end, each purchase of an Acoma Press resource serves to catalyze disciple-making and to equip leaders in God's Church. In fact, a portion of your purchase goes directly to funding planting and replanting efforts in North America and beyond. To see more of our current resources, visit us at *acomapress.org*.

Thank you.

Made in USA - Kendallville, IN
1048492_9781732229167
02.05.2020 0809